Avoiding Spiritual Counterfeiters

Avoiding Spiritual Counterfeiters

by
John MacArthur, Jr.

MOODY PRESS
CHICAGO

© 1988 by
JOHN F. MACARTHUR, JR.

Scripture quotations in chapters 1-3, unless noted otherwise, are from the *New Scofield Reference Bible*, King James Version. Copyright © 1967 by Oxford University Press, Inc. Reprinted by permission.

Scripture quotations in chapter 4, unless noted otherwise, are taken from the *New American Standard Bible*, © 1960, 1962, 1963, 1968, 1971, 1972, 1973, 1975, and 1977 by The Lockman Foundation. Used by permission.

Moody Press, a ministry of the Moody Bible Institute, is designed for education, evangelization, and edification. If we may assist you in knowing more about Christ and the Christian life, please write us without obligation: Moody Press, c/o MLM, Chicago, Illinois 60610.

ISBN: 0-8024-5375-9

1 2 3 4 5 6 7 8 Printing/LC/Year 93 92 91 90 89 88

Printed in the United States of America

Contents

These Bible studies are taken from messages delivered by Pastor-Teacher John MacArthur, Jr., at Grace Community Church in Panorama City, California. The recorded messages themselves may be purchased as a series or individually. Please request the current price list by writing to:

WORD OF GRACE COMMUNICATIONS
P.O. Box 4000
Panorama City, CA 91412

Or call the following toll-free number:
1-800-55-GRACE

1
How to Treat False Teachers—Part 1

Outline

Introduction

The church at Ephesus had a great beginning. Other churches throughout Asia Minor grew out of the Ephesian church. Yet despite the influence of the apostle Paul's ministry, the Ephesian church was never impervious to false teaching. As a result, Paul wrote 1 Timothy to remind Timothy of his responsibility to stop false teachers and set things in order in the church. He commanded Timothy to maintain pure teaching and set an example for other churches to follow.

Paul speaks in verses 3-11 of the necessity of stopping false teachers. Stopping them demands an understanding of four things: their error, their goal, their motive, and their result.

Lesson

I. UNDERSTAND THEIR ERROR (vv. 3-4)

"As I besought thee to abide still at Ephesus, when I went into Macedonia, that thou mightest charge some that they teach no other doctrine, neither give heed to fables and endless genealogies, which minister questions rather than godly edifying which is in faith, so do."

A. The Establishment of the Scene

Paul begins verse 3 by saying, "I besought," words of exhortation. Paul was pleading for Timothy to remain in Ephesus. Timothy was approximately thirty-five years old and had been with Paul for about twenty years. He was a true replica of Paul, as Paul implies in verse 2: "My own son in the faith." Yet apparently he displayed a certain timidity in his character. In addition, displacing church leaders was no easy task. Paul might have anticipated Timothy's reluctance and as a result pleaded for him to stay in Ephesus.

Paul himself started the process of eliminating false teachers. In 1 Timothy 1:20 he mentions Hymenaeus and Alexander, perhaps two of the leading false teachers in Ephesus, whom he "delivered unto Satan, that they may learn not to blaspheme." But Paul had since left for Macedonia (v. 3) to visit the Philippians, and Timothy was faced with the difficult assignment of rebuking false spiritual leaders in the church at Ephesus and perhaps also in the sister churches in the surrounding area.

Paul's first epistle to Timothy does not fit within the the chronology of the book of Acts. Acts ends with Paul's imprisonment in Rome. Many believe Paul was released and then journeyed by ship to Ephesus. On the way he is believed to have visited Colosse, something he had promised Philemon he would do (Philem. 22). It is likely that he traveled to Ephesus from Colosse at the same time Timothy was traveling there from Philippi. They met in Ephesus, at which time Paul dealt with Hymenaeus and Alexander. After surveying the situation, Paul apparently left Timothy behind to go to Philippi (Phil. 2:24). Paul had not been gone long before he wrote this epistle to strengthen Timothy for the difficult task at hand. He also wanted to establish Timothy's authority with the people who would listen to the letter.

B. The Extent of the Command

1. Paul's passionate cry

Although 1 Timothy 1:3-4 is a complete thought, it lacks the grammatical structure to be a complete sentence. The first clause begins with "as" but is never resolved. The translators of the King James Version added "so do" at the end of verse 4 because they believed that the expression was needed to complete the sentence. It is not that Paul was unconcerned about grammar; rather, it was that his heart was exercised over the importance of Timothy's dealing with false teachers. He was making a passionate cry to Timothy to accept his command. He knew Timothy was a genuine child in the faith who would carry out the task through the Spirit's power.

2. Paul's direct command

Further, Paul said, "Charge some that they teach no other doctrine, neither give heed to fables and endless genealogies" (vv. 3-4). Paul was giving Timothy apostolic authority to command the false teachers to stop their teaching. False teachers and their error cannot be dealt with lightly in the church; they must be dealt with immediately and firmly. In actuality Paul was giving Timothy a military command (Gk., *parangellō*). Such a command is not an option; it demands obedience to one's superior.

According to 1 Timothy 3:14, Paul had hoped to go to Ephesus himself. But his writing a second letter to Timothy indicates that he never arrived, and so depended on Timothy to protect the church.

Ephesus: A Key to Asia Minor

Ephesus was a key city—a provincial capital in Asia Minor. The city had been declining economically because the river that ran through the city was depositing silt on the shoreline where it met the sea. Consequently, the city was being forced inland and was losing some of its trade. Still, it remained a significant city during the first century after Christ, primarily because of the Temple of Diana, or Artemis, who was the goddess of fertility. Worship included orgiastic fertility rites. In the midst of such a culture was the church that Paul cared about so passionately.

a) Its audience

Notice in 1 Timothy 1:3 that Paul says to "charge some," referring to certain individuals. The expression seems to indicate that a few men were having a rather wide influence—no doubt not merely in Ephesus, but also in the surrounding areas. It is possible that they were all known by name to Paul and Timothy. But if that were the case, why are their names not mentioned? It may be that the Lord did not want to give them any publicity. But more important, perhaps the Lord did not want to list some and leave others out, who then might feel impervious to any censure. The text does not hint that the false teachers were outsiders, such as were those in Galatia and Corinth who had infiltrated the churches there (Gal. 2:4; 2 Cor. 11:4).

b) Its specifics

    (1) Stop teaching heresy

At the end of verse 3 Paul tells Timothy to command those men "that they teach no other doctrine." That is the translation of a verb in the Greek language used only by Paul in the New Testament. He took the Greek word translated "to teach" (*didaskalia*) and added the word *heteros*, which means "of a different kind." The English word *heterodoxy* means something that is unorthodox. The combination of those two Greek words referred to teaching heresy. Paul wanted the false teachers to stop teaching doctrine that contradicted God's revealed truth.

Apparently the false teachers were using the Word of God as their base. They were twisting and perverting the whole nature of Christian truth.

When Peter preached on the Day of Pentecost three thousand were saved (Acts 2:41). Verse 42 says, "They continued steadfastly in the apostles' doctrine." Years later everyone knew that the substance of revealed truth came through the apostles' doctrine. In 2 Timothy 2:2 Paul says to Timothy, "the things that thou hast heard from me among many witnesses, the same commit thou to faithful men, who shall be able to teach others also." But some at the church in Ephesus had deviated from the truth and were teaching error.

    (2) Stop listening to fables

In 1 Timothy 1:4 Paul elaborates on the nature of their error: "Neither give heed to fables and endless genealogies." Timothy was not to occupy his mind with fables or myths (Gk., *muthos*). In 1 Timothy 4:1 Paul indicates that such legends are

11

in fact "doctrine of demons," manufactured by seducing spirits. The false teachers in Ephesus were much like the Athenians as described in Acts 17:21: "All the Athenians and strangers who were there [on Mars Hill] spent their time in nothing else, but either to tell, or hear some new thing." Apparently the false teachers in Ephesus were introducing new things to tantalize the people, passing off demonically contrived falsehoods as divine truth.

Identifying those fables specifically is difficult, because that information has not been revealed to us. We do not know what they may have been reading into the genealogies or how they were interpreting them. It is enough for us to know that what was being taught was contrary to revealed truth. Nevertheless, we can systematize their error to some extent by surveying Paul's teaching on the subject in the pastoral epistles.

(a) 1 Timothy 1:4—In this verse Paul says that the false teachers were giving themselves to "fables and endless genealogies."

(b) 1 Timothy 1:7—The false teachers were promoting error because they were "desiring to be teachers of the law." Somehow the myths and genealogies were connected to Old Testament law. That leads us to believe that a Jewish orientation existed in their error.

(c) 1 Timothy 4:2-3—These teachers were advocating celibacy and prohibiting marriage. They also were commanding people to abstain from food. To them, true spirituality was found through all kinds of abstinence and self-deprivation.

(d) 1 Timothy 4:7—Here Paul refers to their teaching as "profane and old wives fables," teaching that does nothing but bring about ungodliness.

(e) 1 Timothy 6:4-5—Here the apostle describes the false teacher as "proud, knowing nothing, but doting about questions and disputes of words . . . perverse disputings of men of corrupt minds, and destitute of the truth, supposing that gain is godliness." You will find that the underlying motive of all false prophets is money.

(f) 2 Timothy 2:14—Paul says, "Of these things put them in remembrance, charging them before the Lord that they strive not about words to no profit, but to the subverting of the hearers." Apparently the church was having to deal with those who were taking words out of context and ascribing legendary, allegorical meanings to them. Commentator J. N. D. Kelly observed that "much of the rabbinical Haggadah [consists of] a fanciful rewriting of Scripture. . . . It has also been shown that in post-exilic Judaism there was a keen interest in family trees, and that these played a part in controversies between Jews and Jewish Christians" (*A Commentary on the Pastoral Epistles* [London: Adam & Charles Black, 1963], pp. 44-45). Those who were striving over words were not "rightly dividing the word of truth" (v. 15). They were doing just the opposite: wrongly interpreting it, and therefore wrongly applying it.

That kind of thing has gone on through the years and is still going on today. The subtlety of false teaching is that it uses the Word of God, but in a corrupt manner. False teachers use the Word of God to make money, making merchandise out of people. They twist and pervert Scripture for their own ends.

The following is one bizarre interpretation of Scripture. Pope Gregory the Great of the sixth century wrote a study entitled *Morals on the Book of Job* (Oxford: J. H. Parker, 1844). He said that the patriarch's three friends repre-

sent the heretics, his seven sons represent the
twelve apostles, his seven thousand sheep
represent God's faithful people, and his three
thousand camels represent the depraved
Gentiles. That interpretation has no relation
to the biblical text. Such interpretations were
common in the rabbinical period.

In 2 Timothy 2:16-17 Paul further describes
wrong division of the word of truth as being
"profane and vain babblings; [that will] increase unto more ungodliness. And their
word will eat as doth a gangrene." Verse 18
says that two of the false teachers had erred
from the truth. Then in verse 23 Paul describes their teaching as "foolish and un-
learned questions" that "breed strifes."

(g) 2 Timothy 3:8—Paul says that false teachers
"resist the truth, [are] men of corrupt minds,
[and] reprobate concerning the faith."

(h) 2 Timothy 3:13—Paul describes false teachers
as "evil men and seducers [who] shall become
worse and worse, deceiving, and being deceived."

(i) 2 Timothy 4:3-4—People guided by their lusts
"shall turn away their ears from the truth,
and shall be turned unto fables" given by
false teachers.

(j) Titus 1:10-11, 14, 16—Paul notes that "there
are many unruly and vain talkers and deceivers, specially they of the circumcision" (v. 10).
The false teaching was inspired by the Juda-
izers (cf. Acts 15), although it may have con-
tained some elements of Gentile pagan
philosophy. In verse 11 Paul says that their
"mouths must be stopped, who subvert
whole houses, teaching things which they
ought not, for filthy lucre's [money's] sake."
Again, money is the prime motivator. In verse
14 Paul describes their teaching as "Jewish fa-

bles, and commandments of men, that turn from the truth." Then in verse 16 Paul says, "They profess that they know God, but in works they deny him, being abominable, and disobedient, and unto every good work reprobate."

(k) Titus 3:9-11—Paul cautions Titus to "avoid foolish questions, and genealogies, and contentions, and strivings about the law; for they are unprofitable and vain. A man that is an heretic, after the first and second admonition, reject, knowing that he that is such is subverted, and sinneth, being condemned of himself."

We cannot label the heresy of 1 Timothy 1:4 in any specific way except to say that it was contrary to the truth of God. But one thing we can know from surveying the epistles is that God wants all error to be stopped. It is frightening to look across America today and see church after church full of naive people who will hear false teaching and not be able to recognize it. Apologist Walter Martin once said that the average Jehovah's Witness can outdebate the average Christian in thirty minutes because the Christian doesn't know exactly what he believes or why he believes it. People are being victimized by false teachers because many of the true teachers are not instructing believers about how to recognize false doctrine and keep it from intruding their lives. Sometimes keeping false doctrine away from your life is as simple as turning off the television or radio, throwing away a book, or walking away from someone who communicates false teaching. Mixing sacred truth with myths corrupts the Word of God. The cults have done that for years, and liberal Christianity does it now. We must be ready to deal with false teaching.

Teachers who propagate false doctrine are described in the pastoral epistles as ambitious, avaricious, ignorant, hypocritical, prideful, corrupt, bereft of the truth, defiled, unbelieving, disobedient, and abominable. They have turned aside from the truth and have been made shipwreck of the faith.

The Danger Facing the Church

John 8:44 reminds us that Satan is not only a murderer but is also a liar. One of the manifestations of his lying intent is the proliferation of false teachers who besiege the gospel and the church. In addition we can find warning after warning in the Old Testament against those who teach false doctrine. Jeremiah 23-27 alone has many references to false teachers.

Wherever God establishes the truth, Satan endeavors to sow lies and error. In Matthew 7:15 the Lord tells us, "Beware of false prophets, who come to you in sheep's clothing [the garment of a prophet], but inwardly they are ravenous wolves." Later, in Matthew 24:11, during the Olivet Discourse regarding His second coming, Jesus warns us that many false christs will come. First John 2:18 says, "Even now are there many antichrists." The book of Revelation draws us a clear picture of the consummation of the church age—God's final picture of what will happen on the earth. The last days will be characterized by deception and lies, dominated by the false prophet and the Antichrist.

First Timothy 4:1 reminds us that seducing spirits are loose in the church, teaching demonic doctrines. They speak lies. The apostle Paul warns the Galatian church about false teachers (1:6-7; 3:1). In writing to the church at Colosse (Col. 2:8, 16, 18, 20-23), Paul refutes the teaching that salvation in Christ alone is insufficient.

In a general sense, any student of the Bible is aware that wherever truth is, there also will be the encroachment of error. That is precisely what had happened to the church in Ephesus. The Ephesian church had known the blessing of God as few churches in history will ever know. For three years the apostle Paul had ministered there (Acts 20:31). He had warned the church elders, saying, "I know this, that after my departing shall grievous wolves enter in among you, not sparing the flock. Also of your own selves shall men arise, speaking perverse things, to draw away disciples after them. . . . I commend you to God, and to the word of his grace, which is able to build you up, and to give you an inheritance" (Acts 20:29-30, 32). Paul knew that the church at Ephesus, like any church, would come under attack from lying prophets and teachers. And it did. Every church that stands strongly for the truth will have to deal with those Paul calls corrupters of the Word of God (2 Cor. 2:17). In 2 Corinthians 4:2 he refers to them as handling the Word of God deceitfully.

The subtlety of false teaching is that it uses the Word of God but misrepresents its teaching. Those who teach something explicitly and overtly anti-biblical, anti-Christ, and anti-God pose no real threat to the Christian church. But subtle teaching that appears to be biblical yet pulls unwary souls away from the faith is a great danger to the church.

C. The Effect of the Error

1. An attack on the gospel

First Timothy 1:4 says that the false teachers "minister questions rather than godly edifying which is in faith." They provide speculations instead of truth. They continually stir up useless questions, which creates confusion. The Greek word translated "edifying" (*oikonomia*) means "stewardship," "administration," or "dispensation." It refers to a *modus operandi*—a means of operation. Since it is connected with *theos*, the Greek word translated "God," it refers to the plan of God. Through their questions the false teachers struck a blow at the gospel of saving faith. Therefore, they likely propagated a system of works righteousness or legalism.

The Two Religions of the World

Because of the many religious bodies existing in the world today, people are easily confused. But there are really only two religions in the world: the religion of divine accomplishment (God in Christ accomplished salvation apart from any effort of man) and the religion of human achievement (man attains salvation by something he does). The religion of divine accomplishment is the Christian gospel. Every other religion in the world in one way or another fits into the category of human achievement. Wherever false doctrine

17

strikes a blow at the gospel, it will purport that man in and of himself can please God.

Those who interpret Scripture in light of Jewish legends and fables were propagating a legalistic approach to salvation. That is no different from the Mormons, who claim to believe the Bible. Mormons, however, interpret the Bible in the light of *The Book of Mormon*, *Doctrines and Covenants*, and *The Pearl of Great Price*, books which misrepresent, misinterpret, and confuse Scripture. Similarly, the Christian Scientist erroneously evaluates Scripture by using *Science and Health with Key to the Scriptures*, written by Mary Baker Eddy. Many people rely on their particular teacher or system to reinterpret the Word of God according to their legends and musings.

2. An analysis by Paul

Paul said of anyone preaching another gospel, "Though we, or an angel from heaven, preach any other gospel unto you than that which we have preached unto you, let him be accursed [Gk., *anathema*, "devoted to destruction"]" (Gal. 1:8). False teachers are not to be dealt with lightly, especially when one understands their error. Inevitably their error is an attack on the doctrine of salvation by grace through faith. That is not a trifling matter.

II. UNDERSTAND THEIR GOAL (vv. 5-6)

A. The Commandment (v. 5)

1. The essence of the church (v. 5a)

"Now the end [Gk., *telos*, "the objective, the goal"] of the commandment is love."

God wants to see love in the church. Jesus said the identifying mark of believers is love (John 13:35). The church needs to be marked by people who love the Lord their God with all their heart, soul, mind, and strength, and love their neighbor as themselves (Matt. 22:37-39). First John 4:10-11 says, "Herein is love, not that we loved God, but that he loved us, and sent his Son to be the propitiation for our sins. Beloved, if God so loved us, we ought also to love one another." The pervasive characteristic of Christians is love.

The Greek word translated "love" is *agapē*—the love of choice, of the will. It is self-denying, self-sacrificing love. A person who exemplifies that kind of love will live his life for the benefit of God, for the benefit of other believers, and for the benefit of the lost. Paul wanted Timothy to promote love in the fellowship. And that is not the goal of false teachers.

2. The essence of love (v. 5b)

"Love out of a pure heart, and of a good conscience, and of faith unfeigned."

a) A pure heart

A pure heart is a magnificent Old Testament concept. In Psalm 51:10 David says, "Create in me a clean heart, O God." First Samuel 16:7 reminds us that God looks at the heart, whereas man looks at the outward appearance. Proverbs 23:7 says that as a man thinks in his heart, so is he. The heart is the center of a man's beliefs, convictions, and moral character. It is the center of his spiritual desires and his longings toward God. When the heart is made pure by the washing of regeneration and tends toward obedience (Rom. 6:17), it is a pure heart. And out of that pure heart comes love.

b) A good conscience

The Greek word translated "good" (*agathos*) means "perfect." A good conscience produces pleasure, satisfaction, and a sense of well being. The conscience is your self-judging faculty. It responds to your mind. Your mind is the engine; your conscience is the flywheel. Whatever is in your mind will activate your conscience. And if you have a pure heart, you will have a pure conscience because there won't be anything for your conscience to accuse. Your self-judging faculty will pronounce that all is well. Your conscience will provide you with peace, joy, and freedom from guilt because your heart will be pure. Paul affirmed this truth in his own life when he said, "I exercise myself, to have always a conscience void of offense toward God and toward men" (Acts 24:16). That is not the kind of conscience false teachers have. First Timothy 4:2 says that their conscience has been "seared with a hot iron."

c) A genuine faith

Love also comes out of sincere faith, not the hypocritical faith manifested by false teachers. Faith that has no pretense creates love.

A false teacher has a dirty heart, because it has never been cleansed by the true gospel of faith in Christ. His impure heart triggers a guilty conscience. But his conscience may have reached the point where it is so scarred that it has lost its sensitivity. A false teacher also has hypocritical faith. He's a phony. He wears a mask. That kind of life will never produce the love of God. The goal of the false teacher is not to create an environment of love but to feed his ego and fill his pockets.

B. The Contrast (v. 6)

"From which some, having swerved, have turned aside unto vain jangling."

"Having swerved" and "turned aside" speak of missing the mark and turning off course. False teachers aren't headed for the goal of love; they're headed for the fulfillment of their own lusts. According to 1 Timothy 6:5, their desire is gold. First Timothy 1:7 says that they desire to be considered as teachers of the law, even though they don't understand what they're talking about. That is why Paul referred to their teaching as "vain jangling," which is simply irrelevant noise.

Perverted hearts, scarred consciences, and hypocritical faith will never produce love. Genuine love comes from a pure heart, a good conscience. Sincere faith comes about only in the life that has been transformed by Christ. False religions cannot restrain the flesh, reform a life, or transform a heart. They only make a lot of noise—and tragically it is often a damning noise. That is why Titus 1:11 says their "mouths must be stopped."

Focusing on the Facts

1. Who were the first false teachers eliminated from the church at Ephesus (see p. 8)?
2. What was Timothy's responsibility in Ephesus (see p. 8)?
3. What is significant about the sentence structure of 1 Timothy 1:3-4 (see p. 9)?
4. What kind of authority did Paul grant Timothy in verses 3-4 (see p. 9)?
5. Why was Ephesus a key city in Asia Minor (see p. 10)?
6. How many false teachers were exerting influence in the church at Ephesus? Why do they go unnamed (see p. 10)?
7. Explain the meaning of the Greek verb translated "teach no other doctrine" (see p. 11).
8. What were the false teachers using as the basis of their teaching (see p. 11)?
9. Timothy was not to occupy his mind with what (1 Tim. 1:4; see pp. 11-12)?
10. How did Paul characterize the teaching of false teachers throughout his pastoral epistles (see pp. 12-15)?
11. What does Satan endeavor to do wherever God establishes truth (see p. 16)?
12. What did the apostle Paul warn the Ephesian elders about (Acts 20:20-32; see pp. 16-17)?
13. How is false teaching subtle (see p. 17)?
14. What is the effect of the questions that false teachers stir up (see p. 17)?
15. What are essentially the two religions in the world? What do they teach (see pp. 17-18)?
16. What was Paul's analysis of any teaching that is contrary to the gospel of Christ (Gal. 1:8; see p. 18)?
17. What does God desire to see in the church? Support your answer with Scripture (see pp. 18-19).
18. What three things produce love? Explain each (see pp. 19-20).
19. What is the goal of a false teacher (see p. 20)?

Pondering the Principles

1. Do you know what you believe about the Christian faith—and why? To be all that God wants us to be, and especially to help us to recognize false doctrine, it is imperative that we understand the basics of the Christian faith. Begin a systematic study of the doctrines of Christianity. Three good books to get you started are *What Christians Believe*, written by a collection of biblical scholars (Moody Press), and *Know What You Believe* and *Know Why You Believe*, by Paul E. Little (InterVarsity Press). As you grasp the basics, choose one particular doctrine for further study. When you have a good working knowledge of that doctrine, choose another. The idea is to fulfill 2 Timothy 2:15 in your life. Memorize it before you begin: "Be diligent to present yourself approved to God as a workman who does not need to be ashamed, handling accurately the word of truth" (NASB*).

2. Any true believer desires to fulfill Christ's command in John 15:12: "Love one another, as I have loved you." As we have seen, 1 Timothy 1:5 identifies three essential ingredients that produce love: a pure heart, a clear conscience, and a genuine faith. If your heart is not pure, ask God to cleanse it. Then repent of whatever is making it unclean. If your conscience is accusing you, ask God to help you determine why. As He shows you, confess any sin that becomes clear to you and turn away from it. Finally, ask God to show you any insincerity and hypocrisy that may be in your life. As you make your commitment to the essentials of a pure heart, clear conscience, and genuine faith, you will find yourself exhibiting the love of Christ in your life.

New American Standard Bible.

2
How to Treat False Teachers—Part 2

Outline

Introduction
A. The Theme of the Pastoral Epistles
   1. Its importance to the church
   2. Its importance in the book of Titus
      a) The character of leaders
      b) The ability to communicate truth
B. The Teaching of Matthew 7
   1. The warning against false teachers
   2. The description of false teachers
   3. The product of false teachers

Review
I. Understand Their Error (vv. 3-4)
II. Understand Their Goal (vv. 5-6)

Lesson
III. Understand Their Motive (v. 7a)
IV. Understand Their Effect (vv. 7b-11)
   A. The Ignorance of False Teachers (v. 7b)
   B. The Importance of the Law (vv. 8-11)
      1. It is good (v. 8)
      2. It condemns sinners (vv. 9-10)
         a) A declaration of judgment (v. 9a)
         b) A description of sinners (vv. 9b-10a)
            (1) Separating the pairs
            (2) Defining the pairs
               (a) The first group
                  i) Lawless—disobedient
                  ii) Ungodly—sinners
                  iii) Unholy—profane

     (*b*) The second group
        i) The fifth commandment
        ii) The sixth commandment
        iii) The seventh commandment
        iv) The eighth commandment
        v) The ninth commandment
  c) A doctrine that is sound (v. 10*b*)
3. It is part of the gospel (v. 11)
  a) The glorious gospel
    (1) Defined
    (2) Denied
    (3) Demonstrated
  b) The blessed God
  c) The faithful apostle

Conclusion
A. How Is the Teacher Using Scripture?
B. What Is the Teacher's Goal?
C. What Is the Teacher's Motive?
D. What Is the Teacher's Effect?

Introduction

A. The Theme of the Pastoral Epistles

1. Its importance to the church

Two key Greek words in the epistles to Timothy and Titus are *didaskalia* and *eusebeia*. *Didaskalia* is most frequently translated "doctrine." Of the twenty-one times it is used in the New Testament, fifteen are in these three small epistles. The need for sound doctrine is the main theme. The other word, *eusebeia*, is most often translated "godliness." It appears fifteen times in the New Testament, with ten of those instances being in 1 and 2 Timothy and Titus. Both words are used eight times in 1 Timothy alone. Paul's primary concern was for true doctrine and godly living to be present in the church. And that remains just as essential for the church today.

2. Its importance in the book of Titus

To see how important these two features are, let us look at the book of Titus. You will notice that as Paul outlines the qualifications for church leaders in Titus 1:5-8, he is concerned about holy character and an ability to deal with sound doctrine.

a) The character of leaders

Paul said, "to ordain elders in every city . . . if any be blameless, the husband of one wife, having faithful children not accused of profligacy [ungodly conduct], or unruly. For a bishop must be blameless, as the steward of God, not self-willed, not soon angry [hot-tempered], not given to wine, not violent, not given to filthy lucre, but a lover of hospitality, a lover of good men, sober minded, just, holy, temperate [self-controlled]" (vv. 5-8). That's the character of a godly man. The church is to be led by such men.

b) The ability to communicate truth

In addition, Paul said that the godly leader should hold "fast the faithful word as he hath been taught, that he may be able by sound doctrine both to exhort and to confute the opposers. For there are many unruly and vain talkers and deceivers, specially they of the circumcision, whose mouths must be stopped, who subvert whole houses, teaching things which they ought not, for filthy lucre's sake. One of themselves, even a prophet of their own, said, The Cretans are always liars, evil beasts, lazy gluttons. This testimony is true. Wherefore, rebuke them sharply, that they may be sound in the faith, not giving heed to Jewish fables, and commandments of men, that turn from the truth. Unto the pure all things are pure, but unto them that are defiled and unbelieving is nothing pure; but even their mind and conscience is defiled. They profess that they know God, but in works they deny him, being abominable, and disobedient, and to every good work reprobate. But speak thou the things which become sound doctrine" (Titus 1:9–2:1).

It is essential to recognize the two general qualifications for a pastor: godly living and sound doctrine. When Satan infiltrates a church, he does so through unsound doctrine or ungodly living. Our weapons against his tactics are godliness and truth.

B. The Teaching of Matthew 7

In Matthew 7:13-14 Jesus brings the Sermon on the Mount to a climax with an invitation to enter through the narrow gate onto the narrow way of salvation. After giving the invitation, He warned about the broad road that leads to destruction.

1. The warning against false teachers

Christ then said, "Beware of false prophets" (v. 15). For every true prophet calling people to the narrow way, a multiplicity of false prophets are calling people to the broad way that leads to destruction.

Scriptural Reminders of False Teachers

Christ's warning was not new. Deuteronomy 13:1-5 documents the presence of false teaching during the days of Moses. Isaiah 30:9-14 chronicles its existence in the kingdom of Judah. Many warnings about false teachers appear in Scripture.

1. 2 John 7—John said, "Many deceivers are entered into the world, who confess not that Jesus Christ cometh in the flesh. This is a deceiver and an antichrist."

2. Romans 16:17-18—Paul said, "I beseech you, brethren, mark them who cause divisions and offenses contrary to the doctrine which ye have learned; and avoid them. For they that are such serve not our Lord Jesus Christ but their own body, and by good words and fair speeches deceive the hearts of the innocent." They are dangerous because they claim to be from God and to speak God's Word.

3. Jeremiah 5:31—God said, "The prophets prophesy falsely, and the priests bear rule by their means, and my people love to have it so."

4. Jeremiah 14:14—God said, "The prophets prophesy lies in my name. I sent them not, neither have I commanded them, neither spoke unto them; they prophesy unto you a false vision."

2. The description of false teachers

False teachers are dangerous because their deception is damning. And it comes from that most damning deceiver of all, Satan, who disguises himself as an angel of light and his servants as ministers of righteousness (2 Cor. 11:13-15). Some false teachers are heretics; they openly reject the Word of God and teach contrary to it. Others are apostates; they once followed the faith but have since turned away. There are also deceivers, who pretend to still believe the truth. They want to appear as orthodox, fundamental, evangelical Christians, but they are liars.

3. The product of false teachers

In Matthew 7:16 Jesus says, "Ye shall know them by their fruits." It's not only what they say but also what you see in their lives that matters. A false teacher cannot produce good fruit because evil cannot produce good (v. 17).

False teachers will produce evil fruit, but they will try to hide their bad fruit under ecclesiastical garb or by isolating themselves from accountability. People cannot get near enough to them to see the reality of their lives. Some false teachers hide their evil fruit under a holy-sounding vocabulary or an association with fruitful Christians. Some of them cover their evil fruit with biblical knowledge. But they cannot hide it all the time. If you closely examine a false teacher, you will see his evil fruit.

Review

False teachers had risen up in the church at Ephesus and in surrounding areas as well. Timothy's task was to teach sound doctrine and be an example of godly living. But he also had to put a stop to the false teachers. Paul therefore reminded him of four things.

I. UNDERSTAND THEIR ERROR (vv. 3-4; see pp. 8-18)

II. UNDERSTAND THEIR GOAL (vv. 5-6; see pp. 18-21)

Lesson

III. UNDERSTAND THEIR MOTIVE (v. 7a)

"Desiring to be teachers of the law."

False teachers have a consuming desire to be teachers of God's law, but the remainder of verse 7 tells us that they do not understand it. They don't want to know the law, they don't want to know God, and they don't care about people. They simply want the prestige of being recognized as a teacher.

The motive of a true teacher of God's law is in James 3:1: "Be not many teachers, knowing that we shall receive the greater judgment." He who understands the role of a teacher knows that it is not a place for proud people. But these men were proud. First Timothy 6:3-4 says, "If any man teach otherwise, and consent not to wholesome words, even the words of our Lord Jesus Christ . . . he is proud." They were proud, the opposite of what a true teacher should be (cf. 1 Pet. 5:3, 5-6).

The life and writings of Martyn Lloyd-Jones have been a great inspiration to me. He wrote, "The man who is called by God is a man who realizes what he is called to do, and he so realizes the awefulness of the task that he shrinks from it. Nothing but this overwhelming sense of being called, and of compulsion, should ever lead anyone to preach" (*Preachers and Preaching* [Grand Rapids: Zondervan, 1971], p. 107). To be a servant of

God takes humility along with that compulsion. But the false teachers in the Ephesian church knew neither of those things. They sought an office for the sake of its preeminence. Through their subtle novelties, distorted allegories, strict Judaistic legalism, and self-denying asceticism, they wanted to be exalted as teachers of the law (*nomos didaskalos*). They were on a grand ego trip. They wanted the prestige of the rabbinic role, and they wanted to impose the heresy of salvation by works. Their motive was wrong. They were not compelled to preach in humble servitude; they were seeking preeminence.

IV. UNDERSTAND THEIR EFFECT (vv. 7b-11)

A. The Ignorance of False Teachers (v. 7b)

"Understanding neither what they say, nor that about which they affirm."

The Greek word translated "affirm" (*diabebaioomai*) could be translated "speak dogmatically." Not only did the false teachers say things they didn't understand, but they said them dogmatically as if they were absolute truth. Today many people like them pretend to be teachers of God's truth. But if you know the Word of God and listen closely to what they say, you will discover that they don't understand what they're talking about. Furthermore, they continually and confidently speak dogmatically when they are actually ignorant.

B. The Importance of the Law (vv. 8-11)

1. It is good (v. 8)

"We know that the law is good, if a man use it lawfully."

Even though false teachers misrepresent the law, the law itself remains good. The epitome of their error is to set up the law as a means of salvation. That appeals to men who are proud because they believe in the illusion that by themselves they are good enough to please God. A prideful person thinks he doesn't need a Savior because he believes he can attain God's standard by himself. The law is good when it is used lawfully—but how do you use it lawfully? That is what Paul discusses in the following verses.

2. It condemns sinners (vv. 9-10)

   a) A declaration of judgment (v. 9*a*)

   "Knowing this, that the law is not made for a righteous man."

   The Greek text could well be translated, "Law in general is not made for righteous men." The definite article is absent before "law," making it a general reference, yet one that surely encompasses the Mosaic law. The law is not made for righteous men; it is made to condemn sinners. Romans 3:19-20 says that the law was written so that "every mouth may be stopped, and all the world may become guilty before God. Therefore, by the deeds of the law there shall no flesh be justified in his sight." The law condemns everyone to hell because "there is none righteous, no, not one: there is none that understandeth" (Rom. 3:10-11).

   Not one person can fulfill God's standard on his own. Some Jewish leaders believed they fulfilled it. But in Romans 10:3 Paul says that they were ignorant of God's righteousness and went about establishing their own righteousness. They believed that God was less righteous than He was, and they believed that they were more righteous than they were. They were parading around as if they had met the requirements of the law. But the law isn't for the righteous. As long as anyone believes he is righteous, he will never be saved, because he fails to see that no one can satisfy the demands of the law except Christ.

   b) A description of sinners (vv. 9*b*-10*a*)

   "The law is . . . for the lawless and disobedient, for the ungodly and for sinners, for unholy and profane, for murderers of fathers and murderers of mothers, for manslayers, for fornicators, for them that defile themselves with mankind [homosexuals], for kidnapers, for liars, for perjured persons [perjurers]."

The law is designed to expose sinners for what they are. The law is good, but it is not good news. The law wasn't made for righteous men; it was made for sinners so they could see their sin.

(1) Separating the pairs

To demonstrate his point, Paul isolated sinners into several categories derived from the Ten Commandments (Ex. 20:3-17). The first three pairs—lawless and disobedient, ungodly and sinners, unholy and profane—all refer to the first part of the Ten Commandments, which govern our relationship to God. God commands that we not have any other gods before Him, that we worship Him as the true God, that we make no graven images, and that we remember that He is the only one to be adored and worshiped (vv. 3-5). Then in mentioning murderers, fornicators, homosexuals, kidnapers, and liars, he moves through the second half of the Ten Commandments, which govern our relationship to others.

(2) Defining the pairs

(a) The first group

The first three pairs are assembled with both a negative characteristic and a resulting action.

i) Lawless—disobedient

Lawlessness produces disobedience. Anyone who has no standards will be insubordinate. If you don't believe in the law, you won't pay attention to it. Therefore, the lawless are disobedient.

ii) Ungodly—sinners

Someone who is ungodly doesn't care about God or what is true of God. Therefore he commits sin.

iii) Unholy—profane

An unholy person is irreverent. He is indifferent to God and the duty he should render to God. He has no regard for anything sacred.

The law was made for people who are disobedient, impure, and irreverent to show them what they are. When they match their lives to the law of God, they will see themselves as lawless and disobedient, ungodly and sinful, and unholy and profane.

(b) The second group

Paul then moved to the second group of the Ten Commandments, dealing with man's relationship to man.

i) The fifth commandment

The fifth commandment says, "Honor thy father and thy mother" (Ex. 20:12). In 1 Timothy 1:9 Paul says that the law is made "for murderers of fathers and murderers of mothers." That same commandment is broadened in Exodus 21:15: "He that smiteth his father, or his mother, shall be surely put to death." The law was made for people who break the fifth commandment by not honoring their parents. That encompasses dishonor, murder, and everything in between.

ii) The sixth commandment

The Greek word translated "manslayers" in 1 Timothy 1:9 means "murderers." The term *manslaughter* refers to accidental death, but that is not what Paul had in mind. He was referring to the sixth commandment, which says, "You shall not murder" (Ex. 20:13, NASB).

iii) The seventh commandment

According to 1 Timothy 1:10, the law is also made for "fornicators" (heterosexual sinners) and "for them that defile themselves with mankind" (Gk., *arsenokoitēs*, "homosexuals"). That Greek word is made up of two words: "male" and "marriage bed"—in other words, males in the marriage bed. Fornication and homosexuality violate the seventh commandment of God, which allows for no sexual relationship except that between a man and his wife.

iv) The eighth commandment

The eighth commandment says, "Thou shalt not steal" (Ex. 20:15). In 1 Timothy 1:10 Paul refers to "kidnapers." In his day, one of the most prominent ways men revealed their depravity was in stealing children. A great need for slaves existed, and children were easy prey. Exodus 21:16 and Deuteronomy 24:7 assign the death penalty for those who commit such a crime.

v) The ninth commandment

Then Paul mentioned liars and perjurers as violators of the ninth commandment, which states, "Thou shalt not bear false witness against thy neighbor" (Ex. 20:16).

Paul may have given this list because each of the things on it were characteristic of the false teachers in the Ephesian church. Matthew 7:15-20 warns us that a false teacher may appear like a true shepherd. If the truth were known about his life—if you could remove his ecclesiastical garb and filter out his religious talk—you would find some of the characteristics from 1 Timothy 1:9-10. Perhaps one of the leaders in the Ephesian church had killed his parents or had stolen children and sold them into slavery. Perhaps some were homosexuals. Some may have been liars. Therefore, Paul indicted the false leaders in the Ephesian assembly.

Nothing is wrong with the law. In fact, in Romans 7:7-12 Paul says, "Is the law sin? God forbid. Nay, I had not known sin but by the law; for I had not known coveting, except the law had said, Thou shalt not covet. . . . Apart from the law sin is dead. . . . but when the commandment came, sin removed, and I died. And the commandment, which was ordained to life, I found to be unto death. For sin, taking occasion by the commandment, deceived me, and by it slew me. Wherefore, the law is holy, and the commandment holy, and just, and good." Later, in verse 22, Paul says, "I delight in the law of God after the inward man." The law is good because it's the first half of the gospel: it tells people that they're sinners. The second part of the gospel tells them there is a Savior who has met the demands of the law.

c) A doctrine that is sound (v. 10b)

"And if there be any other thing that is contrary to sound doctrine."

The Greek word translated "sound" is *hugianinō*, from which we derive the English word *hygenic*. It speaks of that which is healthy, is wholesome, and promotes life and health. Paul advocated the kind of teaching that produces spiritual life and growth.

34

3. It is part of the gospel (v. 11)

"According to the glorious gospel of the blessed God, which was committed to my trust."

a) The glorious gospel

    (1) Defined

        Paul affirmed that the law is part of the gospel. What is the gospel? That man is a sinner of such depth and profundity that he cannot redeem himself. But Jesus Christ—God in human flesh—came into the world, died on a cross, and was raised the third day for our justification. Through faith in Him and by the grace of God we can be forgiven of our sins. Thus the law, rightly defined, is part of the gospel. Initially, however, the good news is not good news. The gospel says man is a sinner: he is lost without Christ, and his sin is unforgiven, which damns him forever in an eternal hell.

    (2) Denied

        When people cover up the message of sin, it helps no one. The law is not to be hidden. If someone claims to have a better message than the glorious gospel of the blessed God, then he has no understanding of who God is. I am amazed by the number of people who want to emasculate the law aspect of the gospel. They want to strip out mention of sin, believing they will produce a better gospel than God's glorious one.

    (3) Demonstrated

        The gospel demonstrates God's glory. Part of God's glory is His attributes, some of which are His hatred of sin, His wrath, His judgment, His condemnation, and His holiness. But when those attributes are stripped from the gospel, God becomes nothing more than a benign Santa Claus.

That is not the glorious God or His glorious gospel. People have to see His holy hatred of sin and His condemning justice because those are part of His essential being. Only then can people understand His grace, mercy, and love.

The gospel is called glorious because it is how God's glory is revealed. It begins with the law that damns men to hell, but it ends with forgiven sinners. All that God is comes together in the gospel. It is the gospel of His glory.

b) The blessed God

"The blessed God" doesn't mean that we ascribe blessedness to God; it means that God is the source of blessing. In 1 Timothy 6:15 Paul speaks of the Lord Jesus Christ as "the blessed and only Potentate, the King of kings, and Lord of lords." His very nature is perfect, magnificent, and forever blessed.

c) The faithful apostle

Paul concludes 1 Timothy 1:11 by saying that the glorious gospel of the blessed God was committed to his trust. He didn't receive it from men, but from Christ Himself (Gal. 1:11-12). He wanted to be a faithful steward of the mysteries God had revealed to him (1 Cor. 4:1-2). In 1 Corinthians 9:16 Paul says, "Woe is unto me, if I preach not the gospel!" And in Romans 1:15-17 he says, "As much as in me is, I am ready to preach the gospel to you that are at Rome also. For I am not ashamed of the gospel of Christ." Paul was under a divine commission.

Conclusion

How can we be alert to the infiltration of false teachers? Ask yourself these questions about the Bible teachers you encounter.

A. How Is the Teacher Using Scripture?

Is there error in his understanding of Scripture? Is his interpretation sound, biblical, and legitimate? Don't look at his personality. Don't look at the religious trappings. Don't look only at his associations, although that will tell you something if those associations are negative. Listen to what he says. Do what 1 John 4:1 says: test him to see if he's from God. What is his approach to Scripture? Is he teaching things that go beyond Scripture? Is he saying things that sound good but you can't find verses to support?

B. What Is the Teacher's Goal?

Does he have a spiritual goal? Is his primary desire in life to produce people who consummately love God? Or is he characterized by self-love, self-aggrandizement, possessiveness, and materialism? What is his objective? Is it love for God and for everyone else? Is his objective holiness, a pure heart, a good conscience, and faith without hypocrisy?

C. What Is the Teacher's Motive?

Does he demonstrate a selfless motive? Can you see humility, meekness, and selflessness in his life? Or does it appear that he's helping others to become wealthy? Is he self-indulgent at the expense of the people to whom he is supposed to be ministering?

D. What Is the Teacher's Effect?

Do his followers clearly understand the gospel of Jesus Christ? Do they understand the proper use of the law?

Check his doctrine, his goal, his motive, and his followers. As you do, you'll sense the need for urgency in dealing with false teachers.

Focusing on the Facts

1. What was Paul's primary purpose in writing to Timothy (see p. 24)?

2. In what way did Jesus warn His disciples about the danger of false prophets (see pp. 26-27)?
3. What are some ways that false teachers can be characterized (see p. 27)?
4. What ultimately will expose a false teacher for what he is (see p. 27)?
5. Identify the consuming desire of false teachers (1 Tim. 1:7; see p. 28).
6. What does a genuine teacher of God's Word understand about his role (see p. 28)?
7. What is the true motive behind the consuming desire of false teachers (see p. 29)?
8. How does Paul describe the ignorance of false teachers (1 Tim. 1:7; see p. 29)?
9. How do false teachers misuse the law of God (see pp. 29-30)?
10. Explain how the law of God can be good yet be a bearer of bad news (see pp. 30-31).
11. For what purpose was the law made (see pp. 30-31)?
12. How does Paul describe sinners? Explain each description (1 Tim. 1:9-10; see pp. 30-34).
13. What two relationships do the Ten Commandments govern (see p. 31)?
14. What might have been Paul's reason for giving such an extensive list of negative characteristics in 1 Timothy 1:9-10 (see p. 32)?
15. What is the gospel? Why is it called "glorious" (see pp. 35-36)?
16. Explain the title "the blessed God" (see p. 36).
17. What should a believer do to be alert to the infiltration of false teachers (see pp. 36-37)?

Pondering the Principles

1. The Greek words for doctrine (*didaskalia*) and godliness (*eusebeia*) are each used eight times in 1 Timothy. Look up each of those references: doctrine (1:10; 4:1, 6, 13, 16; 5:17; 6:1, 3) and godliness (2:2; 3:16; 4:7, 8; 6:3, 5, 6, 11). What conclusions can you draw from Paul's use of those words? What personal applications can you make?

2. Review the list of questions on pages 36-37. If you have been concerned about the Bible teaching you or someone you know has been receiving, compare that teacher and his teaching

against that grid. Determine what he is teaching. Ask him what his goals are. Are they spiritual? What is his motive? Finally, do the people that sit under his teaching have a clear understanding of the gospel? If the teacher and his teaching do not appear to pass the test (1 John 4:1), ask him to help you understand the direction of his ministry. If your discussion is fruitless, you may need to remove yourself or help your friend remove himself from that environment (Jude 23).

3
The Pathology of False Teachers

Outline

Introduction

Lesson
I. The Mark of False Teachers (v. 3)
   A. The Difference in Their Teaching
      1. The revealed truth
      2. The subversive element
         a) In the Ephesian church
         b) In every church
   B. The Tests of Their Teaching
      1. What they affirm (v. 3a)
         a) Revealing their error
         b) Recognizing their error
            (1) Acts 20:27
            (2) Ephesians 4:11-14
      2. What they deny (v. 3b)
      3. What they produce (v. 3c)
         a) An examination of false teachers
            (1) Conduct
            (2) Creed
         b) A description of false teachers
            (1) By Peter
            (2) By Jude
II. The Attitude of False Teachers (v. 4a)
III. The Mentality of False Teachers (v. 4b)

Introduction

In 1 Timothy 6:3-5 Paul uses medical terminology to describe false teachers, so I've entitled this chapter "The Pathology of False Teachers." Pathology is the study of the nature and course of disease. False teaching is a deadly disease, and it has an observable pathology. The apostle Paul describes that pathology in 1 Timothy 6:3-5. Paul had already warned Timothy about false teaching in 1 Timothy 1:3-7, 18-20; 4:1-5, and would say more about it in 6:20-21.

First Timothy 6:3-5 describes the internal deviations from spiritual normalcy that characterize false teachers. The pathological characteristics Paul laid out are not unknown to us, but we need to be reminded of them.

One of the duties every pastor, Bible teacher, or spiritual leader has is warning others of error. It isn't enough to be positive and help people see the good side of everything. Warnings run throughout the Old and New Testaments because God knows His people can be led astray by false teaching if they aren't properly prepared. Also, false teaching victimizes those who have never embraced the truth because they come under the illusion that they have found it. We are thus reminded of the danger of false teaching.

Lesson

I. THE MARK OF FALSE TEACHERS (v. 3)

A. The Difference in Their Teaching

Verse 3 begins, "If any man teach otherwise." That's the first pathological characteristic of false teaching: it is teaching different. But different from what?

1. The revealed truth

First Timothy 6:2 says, "These things teach and exhort." That refers to everything Paul has taught in this epistle. In chapter 1 he speaks about a proper understanding of the law of God, the saving gospel, and the majesty of God. In chapter 2 he speaks about praying for the lost and the role of women in the church. In chapter 3 he describes what elders and deacons are to be like. In chapter 4 he teaches about the source of false doctrine and gives principles for an effective ministry. In chapter 5 he instructs Timothy as to how believers should treat older men, older women (particularly widows), and younger widows. Then he discusses how to treat the elders of the church. In the first two verses of chapter 6 he discusses how a slave should serve both a believing and unbelieving master. Paul wanted Timothy to teach the congregation to obey all those things because they were God's revealed truth.

2. The subversive element

In verse 3, when Paul says, "If any man teach otherwise," he means anything that is different from what has been revealed through the inspiration of the Holy Spirit in Scripture.

a) In the Ephesian church

We have already seen that men had infiltrated the church, teaching bizarre fables, endless genealogies, and other things that were not edifying (1:4). They wanted to be teachers of the law but didn't understand what they were teaching (1:7). They were teaching doctrines spawned by seducing spirits (4:1). They were hypocritical liars (4:2). They were teaching people to abstain from things God had "created to be received with thanksgiving" (4:3). They were teaching "profane and vain babblings, and oppositions of knowledge falsely so called" (6:20).

b) In every church

Therefore, when Paul said, "If any man teach otherwise," he knew already that they were doing so. Since he did not mention any specific teacher or teaching, we can conclude this is a generic statement embracing all subversive doctrines and agents of Satan that had infiltrated the church with their deadly virus.

False teachers were rampant in the ancient world. From the beginning, Satan, the father of lies (John 8:44), rebelled against God and began teaching lies. Since then he has been spawning other liars to attack God's truth. Whether facing the false prophets of the Old Testament or the false teachers of the New, the people of God continually have had to do battle against lies and errors. Any church, pastor, or Christian who is not aware of that has his head in

44

the sand. Our Lord said false christs would come. And Scripture is replete with such warnings (see pp. 26-27).

B. The Tests of Their Teaching

1. What they affirm (v. 3*a*)

"If any man teach otherwise."

a) Revealing their error

You have to listen to what they say. Is it different from what you know Scripture says? The Greek word translated "teach otherwise" is *heteros didaskalia*, a heterodox teaching rather than an orthodox teaching. That means it is heresy—something that is different from what Scripture teaches. False teachers do not obtain their teaching from the Word of God—they use something other than the Bible. They may base their teaching on some vision, some revelation, some psychological insight, some self-generated doctrine, or some interpretation contrary to Scripture.

b) Recognizing their error

Since false teachers are marked by teachings that differ from Scripture, we can spot these carriers of spiritual virus and deadly infection by knowing Scripture. First John 2:14 speaks of those who know Scripture as young men, saying, "Ye are strong, and the word of God abideth in you, and ye have overcome the wicked one."

When I began my pastorate at Grace Community Church, two portions of Scripture set the course for my ministry.

(1) Acts 20:27—Paul said, "I have not shunned to declare unto you all the counsel of God." For three years he spent his time night and day going from house to house publicly, and in the meetings of the church on the Lord's Day,

45

teaching the Word and warning the people (v. 31). In verses 29-30 he says why: "I know this, that after my departing shall grievous wolves enter in among you, not sparing the flock. Also of your own selves shall men arise, speaking perverse things, to draw away disciples after them." Then he said, "I commend you to God, and to the word of His grace, which is able to build you up" (v. 32). The only way we can be protected against error is to know truth. False teachers will bring destructive heresies (2 Pet. 2:1) and teach hypocritical lies (1 Tim. 4:1). Those who recognize them are those who know the Word of God. The primary task of the shepherd is to feed the sheep a proper diet so that they won't be tempted by the deadly weeds that grow on the fringes of their pasture.

(2) Ephesians 4:11-14—God has given to the church "apostles; and some, prophets; and some, evangelists; and some, pastors and teachers; for the perfecting of the saints for the work of the ministry for the edifying of the body of Christ, till we all come in the unity of the faith, and of the knowledge of the Son of God, unto a perfect man, unto the measure of the stature of the fullness of Christ; that we henceforth be no more children, tossed to and fro, and carried about with every wind of doctrine, by the sleight of men, and cunning craftiness, by which they lie in wait to deceive." We are to know the Word so that we might be able to discern error.

Ephesians 6:17 says to take "the sword of the Spirit, which is the Word of God." A believer must have the sword to be able to defend himself against the attacks of Satan. In 1 Timothy 4:6 Paul says that a good minister will be "nourished up in the words of faith and of good doctrine." In verse 16 he adds, "Take heed unto thyself and unto the doctrine; continue in them; for in doing this thou shalt both save thyself and them that hear thee." When you and your people know good doctrine, you are protected from the deadly virus of error. The only antibiotic we have against false teaching is the truth of God. Paul reiterated the same point in his second epistle to Timothy: "Hold fast the form of sound words. . . . That good thing which was committed unto thee keep" (1:13-14). "The things that thou hast heard from me among many witnesses, the same commit thou to faithful men, who shall be able to teach others also" (2:2). "Preach the word. . . . For the time will come when they will not endure sound doctrine but, after their own lusts, shall they heap to themselves teachers, having itching ears" (4:2-3).

False teachers are marked by heresy. They affirm things that are different from what Scripture says. They even add things to Scripture.

2. What they deny (v. 3*b*)

"If any man . . . consent not to wholesome words, even the words of our Lord Jesus Christ."

The verb translated "consent not" is in the present tense: the false teacher is not presently in agreement with Scripture. Specifically, they disagree with the "wholesome words of . . . our Lord Jesus Christ." That does not simply refer to what Jesus said in the gospels, but to all He has said as the author of Scripture. Colossians 3:16 calls Scripture "the word of Christ" and 1 Thessalonians 1:8 and 2 Thessalonians 3:1 call it "the word of the Lord."

Scripture provides wholesome, healthy teaching. Peter said, "As newborn babes, desire the pure milk of the word, that ye may grow by it" (1 Pet. 2:2). But false teachers do not heed the life-message that comes from our Lord because they are not committed to Scripture. They may talk about Jesus and God, but the heart of their ministry will not be the Word of God. They will add to it and take away from it.

3. What they produce (v. 3*c*)

"If any man . . . consent not . . . to the doctrine which is according to [related to] godliness."

The ultimate test of a doctrine is whether it produces godliness. Because false teachers ignore God's Word, they do not have godly life-styles. Only the Word of God produces healthy spiritual behavior. That is why 1 Timothy 4:7 says, "Exercise thyself rather unto godliness." Error can never produce godliness.

The term *godliness* speaks of reverence, piety, and Christlikeness. False teaching, heresy, and error cannot produce those virtues. Only the truth of God can.

a) An examination of false teachers

    (1) Conduct

        The life-style of false teachers is telling. In Matthew 7:16 Jesus says, "Ye shall know them by their fruits." Take a look at their conduct. Do they take pleasure in wickedness? Are they lewd (2 Pet. 2:10)? Are they prideful? Are they concerned with prestige, power, and popularity? Are they self-centered and self-indulgent? Such characteristics are not produced by truth but by lies.

    (2) Creed

        Listen to what false teachers say. Are they calling their people to repentance and holiness? Are they urging people to abandon their self-indulgence and be broken over their sin? Or are they teaching doctrines that accommodate the carnal mind and feed the fallenness of man?

b) A description of false teachers

    (1) By Peter

        Second Peter 2 describes their godlessness in vivid terms: they "indulge the flesh in its corrupt desires" (v. 10, NASB). They are daring and self-willed (v. 10). "They count it a pleasure to revel in the daytime. They are stains and blemishes, reveling in their deceptions, as they carouse with you, having eyes full of adultery and that never cease from sin, enticing unstable souls, having a heart trained in greed, accursed children" (vv. 13-14, NASB). "They entice by fleshly desires, by sensuality" (v. 18, NASB). "It has happened to them according to the true proverb, 'A dog returns to its own vomit,' and, 'A sow, after washing, returns to wallowing in the mire' " (v. 22, NASB).

(2) By Jude

Jude said they are "ungodly persons who turn the grace of our God into licentiousness" (v. 4, NASB). They "defile the flesh," caring only for themselves (vv. 8, 12, NASB). Their own shame billows the waves of the sea (v. 13).

II. THE ATTITUDE OF FALSE TEACHERS (v. 4a)

"He is proud."

A false teacher is marked by an attitude of pride. The Greek word translated "proud" (*tuphoomai*—also used in 1 Tim. 3:6) speaks of being engulfed in smoke. Here the perfect passive form is used, indicating that false teachers are in a settled state of being engulfed in their own smoke.

False teachers are invariably arrogant. When someone claims his teaching is superior to the Word of God, that is the epitome of arrogance. An arrogant person is inflated with his own sense of self-importance. Peter said false teachers are so arrogant that "they do not tremble when they revile angelic majesties" (2 Peter 2:10, NASB). Rather, they speak "out arrogant words of vanity" (2 Pet. 2:10, NASB). Jude said that they reject authority (v. 8) and speak arrogantly (v. 16). Anyone who puts his teaching above the Word of God is arrogant. False teachers refuse to accept the straightforward truth of God. They may try to pass themselves off as humble, meek, and self-effacing, but to affirm teaching contrary to the Word of God is the height of arrogance. Should we expect any less of them if Satan is their example? In his arrogance the false teacher chooses to be greater than God, and as a result he spawns a generation of sinners with the same desire.

For example, Simon, the sorcerer, purposed that he was a great person (Acts 8:9). People who are inflated with their own sense of self-importance are nothing more than deviants revealing the pathology of their virus.

III. THE MENTALITY OF FALSE TEACHERS (v. 4b)

A. In Principle

"Knowing nothing."

It doesn't matter how many Ph.D.'s or how much training false teachers have; they still don't know the truth (1 Tim. 1:7). But they are inflated over what they think they know. They parade their imagined intelligence, scholarship, superior understanding, deeper insights, and religious acumen, but they are ignorant.

1. Characterized

In 1 Corinthians 3:19 Paul says, "The wisdom of this world is foolishness with God." False teachers do not have insight into any matter of spiritual truth. They have wisdom that is not from above, but that which is earthly, sensual, and demoniac (James 3:15). They may claim to have some new truth or insight, but they do not.

The Lord has chosen to hide "these things from the wise and prudent, and hast revealed them unto babes" (Matt. 11:25). God has hidden His truth from the self-promoting minds of this world and given it to those who believe His Word.

2. Classified

a) By Peter

Second Peter describes their ignorance in strong terms. It speaks of false teachers as "unreasoning animals, born as creatures of instinct to be captured and killed, reviling where they have no knowl-

50

edge" (2 Pet. 2:12, NASB). In verse 17 of the same chapter they are called "springs without water"—they promise to quench your thirst but are as dry as a sand pit.

b) By Jude

Jude says that false teachers are "clouds without water, carried along by winds; autumn trees without fruit, doubly dead, uprooted; wild waves of the sea, casting up their own shame like foam; wandering stars" (vv. 12-13, NASB).

B. In Practice

"Doting about questions and disputes of words."

The Greek text could be translated "having a sick craving for questions and word battles." False teachers have a disease—a morbid preoccupation with useless questions and word battles. They make a fuss about terminology. The Greek word translated "questions" (*zētēsis*) means "idle speculations." It is nothing more than pseudo-intellectual theorizing. They make a fuss about theory instead of the truth of God's Word. So much is written about Scripture from a liberal or neoorthodox viewpoint. It's easy to get lost in all the verbiage and speculation. Yet all you need to do is accept the plain truth of God's Word.

False teachers also get into "disputes of words" (Gk., *logomachia*, "word battles"). They battle each other over terminology. Their minds know nothing, so they fight over semantics.

IV. THE EFFECTS OF FALSE TEACHERS (vv. 4c-5a)

"Of which cometh envy, strife, railings, evil suspicions, perverse disputings of men of corrupt minds."

Godliness is the ultimate test of truth. But there's a second one: unity. That which unites believers is a common commitment to the truth.

A. The Perversion of Unity

False teachers teach their own thing—whatever is right in their own eyes. They will either add their material to Scripture, or they will deny Scripture in favor of what they teach. Because each ego-motivated doctrine becomes their own particular standard, such teachers become pitted against one another. And that results in discord and chaos. When students go to schools that teach false doctrine, or sit under that kind of teaching, they became confused because there's no uniformity among error.

B. The Path of Discord

1. Envy

Jealousy is inward discontent over someone else's popularity and prosperity. One teacher teaches one false doctrine, another teaches his, and they are both jealous over the other's success.

2. Strife

Strife describes the ensuing battle between them.

3. Slander

Insults and slander are a by-product of strife and jealousy.

4. Suspicion

A factious person tends to suspect others of evil motives.

5. Bickering

The Greek word translated "perverse disputings" (*diaparatribai*) speaks of something in constant friction. In his homily on 1 Timothy 5:2-7, the fourth-century church Father John Chrysostom said that false teachers were like infected sheep coming into contact with others and thereby spreading their disease.

The legacy of error is chaos—one errorist pitted against another, jealously fighting, blaspheming, insulting one another, suspicious of one another's motives, creating nothing but constant friction. They produce nothing good at all.

C. The Product of Error

1. According to Peter

Peter said that because of them "the way of the truth will be maligned; and in their greed they will exploit you with false words" (2 Pet. 2:2-3, NASB). They will entice unstable souls. They promise freedom but are the slaves of corruption (v. 19).

2. According to Jude

Jude said that they are like unreasoning animals who follow their depraved instincts to destruction (v. 10). They rush headlong into error, traveling the path of self-centered disobedience, and they perish in their own rebellion (v. 11). Verse 12 describes them as "hidden reefs" (NASB).

False teachers cause chaos because error can never produce unity. Only truth unifies.

V. THE CAUSE OF FALSE TEACHERS (v. 5b)

"Men of corrupt minds."

False teachers have unregenerate minds—minds that have never been transformed. In Romans 8:7 Paul says that their "carnal mind is enmity against God." Their minds are filled with earthly wisdom that fights against God (James 3:15; 4:4). In Romans 1:28 Paul says, "God gave them over to a reprobate mind." Their mental faculties do not function properly in the moral or spiritual realm. They do not react positively to truth. In 1 Corinthians 2:14 Paul calls them natural men who "receiveth not the things of the Spirit of God." The pathological source of their disease is a corrupt mind. The deadly virus of ignorant, damning words comes out of an evil mind. They don't understand God, and they can't understand truth.

Ephesians 4:18 says that their understanding is darkened and alienated from God. Colossians 1:21 says that they are "alienated and enemies in [their] mind by wicked works."

False teachers possess alienated, wicked, darkened, and corrupt minds. Such teachers have been transformed. They have not received the mind of Christ (1 Cor. 2:16). They may have many theological degrees and may be involved in religious activities, but their minds are corrupt.

VI. THE CONDITION OF FALSE TEACHERS (v. 5c)

"Destitute of the truth."

A. Destitute of the Truth

False teachers are bereft of the truth. The Greek word translated "destitute" comes from a verb that means "to steal" or "to deprive." False teachers have been deprived of the truth.

1. In the middle voice

The Greek word translated "destitute" could be in the middle voice or in the passive voice. The forms of the word are the same. If used as a middle-voice verb, "destitute" would indicate that they were in contact with the truth but willfully deprived themselves of it. That doesn't mean they were ever saved, but that they did know the truth and moved away from it.

2. In the passive voice

If the Greek word is taken in the passive voice the meaning is that someone took the truth from them. Perhaps they came under the influence of someone who pulled them away from truth. It is important that we warn people to be careful to whom they listen and what they read so that they don't become victimized.

These false teachers once had contact with the truth. But now they had been deprived of it, or had deprived them-

selves of it. They could be "those who were once enlightened" (Heb. 6:4) but then had abandoned what they once
knew. Therefore, we would call their condition apostasy
—they departed from the faith.

B. Departed from the Truth

To whom have these men been listening? The father of
lies, Satan himself (John 8:44). Second Timothy 2:18 says
that they have erred concerning the truth, being "men of
corrupt minds, reprobate concerning the faith" (3:8).

VII. THE PROGNOSIS OF FALSE TEACHERS

The prognosis of false teachers is implied in the statement
"destitute of the truth": judgment. Anyone who is bereft of
the truth is headed for judgment. Hebrews 6:6 tells us that if
anyone turns away from the truth, there is no hope of his being saved. Hebrews 10:29 says that those who trample under
their feet the Son of God and consider the blood of the covenant an unholy thing are headed for eternal judgment.

A. By Peter

Second Peter 2 says that false teachers bring "swift destruction on themselves. . . . Their judgment from long
ago is not idle, and their destruction is not asleep. For if
God did not spare angels when they sinned, but cast
them into hell and committed them to pits of darkness,
reserved for judgment; and did not spare the ancient
world, but preserved Noah . . . when he brought a flood
upon the world of the ungodly, and if He condemned the
cities of Sodom and Gomorrah to destruction by reducing
them to ashes . . . then the Lord knows how . . . to keep
the unrighteous under punishment for the day of judgment" (vv. 1, 3-6, 9, NASB).

B. By Jude

The book of Jude is direct. It says that false teachers were
"of old ordained to this condemnation" (v. 4). Verse 15
says that God is going "to convict all that are ungodly
among them of all their ungodly deeds which they have

ungodly committed, and all their hard speeches which ungodly sinners have spoken against him."

The prognosis of false teachers is judgment. They will experience the severest hell, because after having seen the truth, they apostatized from it.

VIII. THE MOTIVE OF FALSE TEACHERS (v. 5d)

"Supposing that gain is godliness."

The King James Version adds the phrase "from such withdraw yourself," but earlier manuscripts do not include it. False teachers teach their doctrines to receive money. They have the audacity to presume that their "godliness"—their false piety—is a way to make money.

A. Shunning the Temptation

In Acts 20:29 Paul says, "I know this, that after my departing shall grievous wolves enter in among you." Then in verses 32-33 he says, "I commend you to God, and to the word of his grace, which is able to build you up, and to give you an inheritance among all them who are sanctified. I have coveted no man's silver, or gold, or apparel." Why? Because false teachers were in the ministry to fleece the people, not feed the sheep. Paul wasn't like that. He told the Corinthians that he didn't expect anything from them (1 Cor. 9:4-18). He told the Thessalonians he didn't want to be a burden to them—so he worked with his hands to provide his own living (1 Thess. 2:9).

B. Succumbing to Temptation

In 1 Timothy 3 Paul says that an elder and a deacon cannot be covetous and a lover of money because the potential to use religion to make money has always been the motivation of false teachers (vv. 3, 8).

1. Balaam

Second Peter 2:3 says, "In their greed they will exploit you" (NASB). Verse 15 says that they have "followed the way of Balaam, the son of Beor, who loved the wages of unrighteousness" (NASB). Balaam was a prophet who would give a message to the highest bidder. Jude says, "They have rushed headlong into the error of Balaam" (Jude 11, NASB). They flatter "people for the sake of gaining an advantage" (v. 16, NASB).

2. Simon

   In Acts 8:18-19 Simon wanted to buy the Holy Spirit. He would have paid anything he could to buy the power he saw revealed. He knew if he possessed that power he could make back what he had spent and a thousand other fortunes. Religious charlatans are a steady parade in this society and are in it for the money.

Stay away from people who teach doctrine contrary to Scripture. Stay away from those who deny the truth. Stay away from those who are not Christlike and godly in their conduct. Don't listen to those who are arrogant, ignorant of spiritual reality, and the makers of useless speculations. Those things generate word battles that lead to chaos, confusion, disorder, and disunity. Stay away from those with corrupt minds who have forsaken the truth and are headed for eternal judgment. Stay clear of those who are desirous of personal enrichment at your expense. They are diseased, and the prognosis for them and those they infect is terminal.

Focusing on the Facts

1. How does pathology relate to false teachers (see p. 42)?
2. What is the first pathological characteristic of a false teacher (see p. 43)?
3. What things did Paul want Timothy to teach and exhort (1 Tim. 6:2; see p. 43)?
4. What does the phrase "if anyone teaches differently" embrace (1 Tim. 6:3; see p. 44)?
5. What do people in the church continually face (see p. 44)?
6. How can a believer spot false teachers and their teaching (see p. 45)?
7. What are the "words of our Lord Jesus Christ" (1 Tim. 6:3; see p. 47)?
8. What is the ultimate test of any doctrine (see p. 48)?

9. What two things should a believer examine when trying to determine if someone is a false teacher (see p. 48)?
10. Describe the arrogance of a false teacher (see pp. 48-49).
11. How did Paul characterize the wisdom of the world (1 Cor. 3:19; see p. 50)?
12. According to 1 Timothy 6:4, what is the preoccupation of false teachers (see p. 51)?
13. What is another test of truth in addition to godliness (see pp. 51-52)?
14. What is the path to discord? Explain (see p. 52).
15. What kind of minds do false teachers possess (1 Tim. 6:5; see pp. 53-54)?
16. What is the condition of false teachers (1 Tim. 6:5; see p. 55)?
17. What is the prognosis for false teachers (see pp. 55-56)?
18. What motivates a false teacher to perpetuate his false doctrine (1 Tim. 6:5; see pp. 56-57)?

Pondering the Principles

1. A crucial test of anyone's doctrine is whether it produces godliness. When people live their lives based on the truths of Scripture, they will live godly lives. If someone were to examine the conduct of your life, would he or she conclude that you are committed to the truths of Scripture? Read 1 Timothy 4:7-8. What kind of effort must you give toward living a godly life? Are you putting forth that effort? According to verse 8, what should motivate you to be godly? Examine your own motivations. Be honest with yourself. Is there anything you are holding onto that is preventing you from becoming more godly? If so, let go of it. Ask God to forgive you, and begin from this day forward to discipline yourself for godliness.

2. False teachers typically display wisdom that is earthly, sensual, and demonic (James 3:15). Believers should exhibit wisdom from above. Read James 3:17-18. List each characteristic of heavenly wisdom. Next to each one, evaluate yourself on how well you exhibit that particular characteristic. Choose one that you manifest the least. Look up other Scripture verses on that particular characteristic. Ask God to show you what you need to do to better exhibit that characteristic of wisdom in your life. Once you know what you should do, be faithful to do it.

4
The Danger of False Teaching

Outline

Introduction

Lesson
 I. Reminding True Teachers (v. 14*a*)
 II. Avoiding False Teaching (vv. 14*b*-19)
   A. It Ruins the Hearers (v. 14*b*)
     1. The seriousness of the command
       a) A constant reminder
       b) A healthy fear
         (1) 1 Timothy 5:21
         (2) 1 Timothy 6:13-14
         (3) 2 Timothy 4:1
     2. The specifics of the command
       a) The rejection of word battles
         (1) Satan's strategy
         (2) The church's legacy
       b) The result of word battles
   B. It Shames the Teachers (v. 15)
     1. The key word
     2. The key response
       a) Be diligent
       b) Present yourself approved to God
       c) Be a hard worker
       d) Handle the word of truth accurately
         (1) The method
           (*a*) Its pattern
           (*b*) Its principle

Introduction

Scripture clearly affirms that God is truth, that God speaks truth, and that God cannot lie. Scripture also affirms that Satan is a liar and the father of lies. He is in the business of deceiving people. God reveals Himself as truth, and Satan is revealed as its antithesis. That particular dichotomy pervades every area of the universe. A conflict exists between the holy angels and the unholy demons. There is conflict on earth between the truth of God and the lies of Satan.

The people of God have always been plagued with false doctrine. They have endured the invasion of false prophets and teachers throughout the ages. Satan attempts to confuse the world by drowning it in a sea of deceit. Satan's misrepresentation of the truth to Eve plunged the human race into sin (Gen. 3:1-6). The steady stream of false teaching has been so cumulative that it is wider and deeper now than it has ever been. False teaching about God, Christ, the Bible, and spiritual reality is pandemic. The father of lies works overtime to destroy the saving, sanctifying truth God has given to us in His Word. The effects of false teaching have been devastating and damning. That is why the Bible calls false teachings destructive heresies (2 Pet. 2:1). I believe that as we get closer to the coming of Christ, these deceptions, lies, and misrepresentations will increase.

Any servant of the Lord must be aware of false teachers and warn others about their lies. That is why the apostle Paul warned the believers and leaders in Ephesus (Acts 20:29-30).

Second Timothy 2:14-19 specifically tells us why we should avoid false teaching. Paul had called Timothy to be a faithful servant of the Lord. He asked him to rise above the influence of ungodliness, evil teaching, and evil people, and to set the church right. To do so Timothy would have to keep his mind on the truth of God and be sure that he and his people avoided the impact of false teaching.

Lesson

I. REMINDING TRUE TEACHERS (v. 14a)

"Remind them of these things."

The literal translation would read, "Remind of these things." The word *them* was added because it identifies who is being reminded—the faithful men of verse 2. What things were they to be reminded of? The things that Paul had just said in verses 1-13. Paul wanted Timothy to remind the church leaders and teachers of their responsibility to pass the truth on to others. They needed to be reminded of the noble cause they served and the loftiness of the gospel ministry.

II. AVOIDING FALSE TEACHING (vv. 14b-19)

A transition takes place from Paul's positive reminder to his negative command. In verse 14 he says, "Solemnly charge them." Timothy was not just to continually remind the people of the noble cause they served, but was also to "solemnly charge [Gk., *diamarturomai*, a legal term] them in the presence of God not to wrangle about words." The positive aspect shows the believer what to do; the negative tells him what not to do.

A. It Ruins the Hearers (v. 14*b*)

"Solemnly charge them in the presence of God not to wrangle about words, which is useless, and leads to the ruin of the hearers."

1. The seriousness of the command

   a) A constant reminder

   The Greek word translated "solemnly charge" communicates the idea of a constant reminder and a constant command. Timothy was to constantly remind the leaders of their positive duty and to constantly warn them to avoid false teaching. The warning is serious because *diamarturomai* refers to a solemn command.

   b) A healthy fear

   Paul's solemn command is made even more serious by the next phrase in verse 14, "Solemnly charge them in the presence of God." The leaders were to do their duty out of a healthy fear of God. Paul had given such charges before:

   (1) 1 Timothy 5:21—"I solemnly charge you in the presence of God and of Christ Jesus and of His chosen angels, to maintain these principles without bias."

   (2) 1 Timothy 6:13-14—"I charge you in the presence of God, who gives life to all things, and of Christ Jesus, who testified the good confession before Pontius Pilate, that you keep the commandment without stain or reproach."

   (3) 2 Timothy 4:1—"I solemnly charge you in the presence of God and of Christ Jesus, who is to judge the living and the dead, and by His appearing and His kingdom: preach the Word."

   Those are all serious commands. They are not just commands but solemn commands, and not just solemn commands but solemn commands in the presence of God. The intention of the solemn charge is to put fear in the hearts of God's people by reminding them that they are directly accountable to God.

Exploring the Presence of God

1. As a comforting reality

   a) Psalm 68:8—"The heavens also dropped rain at the presence of God."

   b) Luke 1:19—The angel told Zacharias, "I am Gabriel, who stands in the presence of God; and I have been sent to speak to you, and to bring you this good news."

   c) Hebrews 9:24—"Christ did not enter a holy place made with hands, a mere copy of the true one, but into heaven itself, now to appear in the presence of God for us."

   d) Genesis 27:7—Isaac said, "Bring me some game and prepare a savory dish for me, that I may eat, and bless you in the presence of the Lord."

2. As a means of judgment

   The presence of God is meant to comfort. But the vast majority of references have to do with judgment.

   a) Psalm 68:2—"As wax melts before the fire, so let the wicked perish before God."

   b) Genesis 3:8—Adam and his wife hid themselves after they had sinned so that they wouldn't have to face the presence of God.

   c) Psalm 97:5—"The mountains melted like wax at the presence of the Lord, at the presence of the Lord of the whole earth."

   d) Psalm 114:7—"Tremble, O earth, before the Lord, before the God of Jacob."

e) 2 Thessalonians 1:9—"[Unbelievers] shall be punished with everlasting destruction from the presence of the Lord, and from the glory of his power" (KJV*).

Although there are times when the presence of the Lord is meant to comfort us, it is more often meant to increase our sense of accountability. We are always in the presence of God, and His presence acts as a controlling factor on how we live. He monitors each of our lives. A solemn charge in the presence of God makes its recipients accountable before the Holy One, the righteous judge.

2. The specifics of the command

Given such a serious command, you would expect Paul to name some vile evil from which Timothy was to command the people to withdraw. But Paul says, "Solemnly charge them in the presence of God not to wrangle about words."

a) The rejection of word battles

The Greek word translated "wrangle about words" speaks of waging a war of words. Paul called for the leadership to avoid futile debates because such debates would sidetrack them. Evidently the errorists in Ephesus tended to focus on worthless chatter based on speculation and not on the Word of God (1 Tim. 1:3-4; cf. 1 Tim. 6:3-10). Timothy was not to be drawn into word battles because they were not based on God's special revelation.

(1) Satan's strategy

C. S. Lewis's book *The Screwtape Letters* tells of an older demon, Screwtape, writing to a younger demon, Wormwood, about how to be effective in dealing with people. In his first letter Screwtape says, "Your man has been accustomed, every since he was a boy, to have a dozen incompatible philosophies dancing about together inside his head. He doesn't think of doctrines as primarily

*King James Version.

'true' or 'false,' but as 'academic' or 'practical'.
. . . Jargon, not argument, is your best ally in
keeping him from the Church" ([New York: Mac-
millan, 1961], p. 8). Demons know that true
science and reason will not contribute to their
cause, which is deception. From their point of
view, speculations—not facts—must fill men's
minds. Cunning demons will use that strategy
because it obscures biblical truth by focusing on
temporal concerns.

(2) The church's legacy

Such jargon has infiltrated many of today's col-
leges and seminaries. Also, many television
evangelists and preachers barrage the church
with jargon about their false religious systems. It
has had an effect. How else can you explain why
some churches have reached the point where
they advocate abortion, women preachers, homosexuality, and divorce for any reason? Why
has the church allowed unholy leaders to remain
in leadership? How it is that husbands no longer
lead their homes, and wives have little commitment to the lives of their children? How could the
church ever buy into the self-esteem movement
at the expense of humility and service to others?
Jargon has invaded the church. That is because
the church is willing to listen to the world. It is
willing to put the Bible alongside the reason of
man. In 2 Timothy 2:14 Paul calls the world's jargon useless. Worse than that, it is demonic. First
Timothy 4:1-2 speaks of doctrines spawned by
demons spoken through hypocritical liars.

b) The result of word battles

Paul said these word battles lead to the ruin of the
hearers. The Greek word translated "ruin" (*katastrophē*) means "to overturn," "to subvert," "to upset," or "to overthrow." False teaching doesn't edify;
it tears down. It doesn't strengthen; it weakens.

Katastrophē is used only one other time in the New Testament—in 2 Peter 2:6—which gives us insight into the kind of ruin Paul was referring to. Peter said that God "condemned the cities of Sodom and Gomorrah to destruction [*katastrophē*] by reducing them to ashes." There *katastrophē* means "total devastation." Paul uses it in the same sense in 2 Timothy 2:14—word battles totally destroy the hearers. They lead to the damnation of people's eternal souls. That is why 2 Peter 2:1 calls them destructive heresies that bring about swift destruction. Second Peter 3:16 says, "The untaught and unstable distort [Paul's teaching], as they do also the rest of the Scriptures, to their own destruction." We are called to stay away from false teaching because it has the potential of damning the eternal souls of those under its influence.

B. It Shames the Teachers (v. 15)

"Be diligent to present yourself approved to God as a workman who does not need to be ashamed, handling accurately the word of truth."

1. The key word

The key word is "ashamed." Anyone who teaches anything other than what accurately reflects the word of truth ought to be ashamed. Shame is the painful feeling that arises from an awareness of having done something dishonorable. Anyone who propagates false teaching has reason to be ashamed when he faces God. False teaching is worthy of condemnation by God, not commendation. It doesn't matter to God how many degrees a false teacher has or how erudite he might be. He has every reason to stand before God in shame for mishandling God's precious Word.

2. The key response

a) Be diligent

If you are a teacher, how do you avoid being ashamed before the Lord? Second Timothy 2:15 says, "Be diligent" (Gk., *spoudazō*, "to give diligence," "to

66

give maximum effort," or "to do your best"). Teaching God's Word requires maximum effort. That is why 1 Timothy 5:17 says, "Let the elders who rule well be considered worthy of double honor, especially those who work hard at preaching and teaching." It is hard work.

b) Present yourself approved to God

The Greek word translated "present yourself" in 2 Timothy 2:15 (*paristēmi*) means "to stand alongside." You should desire to stand alongside God.

Paul then said, "Present yourself approved." The Greek word translated "approved" means "proved to be worthy after testing." What is the goal of the teacher? To make a maximum effort so that he might someday stand alongside God unashamed because he has proved himself to be worthy. Paul told the Galatians that he was not a manpleaser (1:10-11). The goal of the apostle Paul was to please God. In 1 Thessalonians 2:4 he says, "Just as we have been approved by God to be entrusted with the gospel, so we speak, not as pleasing men but God, who examines our hearts." The teacher who stands before the Lord and hears the commendation "Well done, good and faithful servant" is one who made a maximum effort.

c) Be a hard worker

The Greek word translated "workman" (*ergatēs*) communicates the idea of energy. It refers to a worker or laborer, not a student. The hard worker is committed to maximum effort so that he might come before his master and show him that his work is worthy. As a result he "does not need to be ashamed."

d) Handle the word of truth accurately

In 2 Timothy 2:15 Paul says, "to handle accurately the word of truth." The literal meaning of the Greek word translated "handling accurately" (*orthotomeō*) is cutting a straight line.

(1) The method

    (*a*) Its pattern

        Orthotomeō was used to refer to any task that required a straight line. For example, it was used of cutting a straight line with a saw. It was used of making a straight path through woods or mountains. It was used of building a building, when a straight edge needed to be cut on stone to be sure that the building was built level. It was used of cutting a straight line on cloth. It was used of cutting straight lines on hides so that they could be pieced together to make a tent.

        Paul was a leather worker. We often say he was a tentmaker, but a better translation of the Greek word is leather worker. He used animal hides, skins, and perhaps woven hair to make things, possibly tents. You can imagine that anyone making a tent would have to piece together a lot of hides. He would have cut each one just right so that he could fit the hides together. It would be similar to dressmaking. If the pieces aren't cut correctly from the pattern, the dress won't look or fit right.

    (*b*) Its principle

        If you don't know how to cut the pieces, you can't make the whole product fit. The same is true in the spiritual realm—biblical theology and exegesis are interdependent. Every teacher must be committed to handling accurately (cutting straight) the Word of truth.

(2) The message

    "Word of truth" (2 Tim. 2:15) is a phrase used other times in Scripture.

    (*a*) Ephesians 1:13—"After listening to the message of truth, the gospel of your salvation."

The message or word of truth refers to the gospel.

> (*b*) James 1:18—"He [God] brought us forth by the word of truth."

> (*c*) John 17:17—Jesus said, "Thy word is truth." Here the word of truth refers to all of God's revelation.

When you realize the importance of handling the gospel correctly, you've got to acknowledge that there is a lot of preaching today that doesn't. We have to handle the Word accurately so that we don't misrepresent the gospel. We have to represent all the Word of God, not in a flippant, offhanded way, but in the proper way. That requires diligence and a desire to be approved by God, not men. It demands that you be a workman.

C. It Leads to Ungodliness (v. 16)

"But avoid worldly and empty chatter, for it will lead to further ungodliness."

1. The degeneration of empty talk

The Greek word translated "avoid" means "to walk around" or "to keep clear of." What are we to avoid? Chatter—jargon of human wisdom apart from God's revelation. Paul called it "worldly [Gk., *bebēlos*, "common, not set apart"] chatter." It is the common, profane, unholy talk of men.

He also called it "empty," which means it has no benefit—it yields no return. But empty words soon become evil words because empty words are like a vacuum. Once in a while when I vacuum my car the vacum cleaner sucks up something I don't want it to, such as a pen or a coin. That's what happens with a vacuum—whatever is near rushes in. Empty words become evil words because they suck up sin. Useless talk on useless matters becomes wicked talk. Words that are not of God soon become unholy words.

69

2. The result of empty talk

False teachers claim to be advancing our thinking, expanding our minds, and leading us to new truth. But actually what they are saying "will lead to further ungodliness" (v. 16). False teachers are ungodly, and they pull down into ungodliness those who hear them. Peter said "many will follow their sensuality" (2 Pet. 2:2). Ungodly conduct is always the fruit of ungodly doctrine.

D. It Spreads Like Gangrene (v. 17*a*)

"Their talk will spread like gangrene."

Gangrene is dead flesh. The bacterial kind spreads fast. The Greek word translated "gangrene" (*gangraina*) can refer to a spreading, consuming disease. To cure gangrene, the patient is sometimes placed in a hyperbaric chamber so that the affected tissues can be exposed to oxygen at high pressure, thereby killing the bacteria, which need an oxygen-free environment. The patient is then treated with antibiotics. Gangrene is like a prairie fire. Jude 23 tells us to "save others, snatching them out of the fire." False teaching is a malignancy—it eats up the neighboring tissue and spreads its corrupting doctrine to infect others.

E. It Can Lead to Apostasy (vv. 17*b*-18)

1. The definition of apostasy (vv. 17*b*-18*a*)

"Among them are Hymenaeus and Philetus, men who have gone astray from the truth."

Hymenaeus and Philetus were apostates, having erred from the truth—like those referred to in Hebrews 6:4-6: "In the case of those who have once been enlightened and have tasted of the heavenly gift and have been made partakers of the Holy Spirit, and have tasted the good word of God and the powers of the age to come, and then have fallen away, it is impossible to renew them again to repentance." That is because in essence

70

they "trampled under foot the Son of God, and . . . regarded as unclean the blood of the covenant by which [they were] sanctified, and . . . insulted the Spirit of grace" (Heb. 10:29).

2. The error of apostasy (v. 18*b*)

"Saying that the resurrection has already taken place."

These apostates probably believed that the resurrection was nothing more than some mystical experience one had when one went from the unenlightened life to the enlightened life. They were probably buying into a philosophical heresy that was prevalent at the time.

A denial of the resurrection is a major error. In 1 Corinthians 15:13-14 Paul says that if there were no resurrection of the dead, then Christ never rose. And if Christ never rose, then neither will we. A doctrine that denies the resurrection cuts the heart out of the gospel. It is a denial of eternal life in a glorified body like Christ's—the essence of the Christian hope.

3. The effect of apostasy (v. 18*c*)

"Thus they upset the faith of some."

The Greek word translated "upset" literally means "to overturn." The people whose faith was overturned obviously had a nonsaving faith. That is because no one can overturn real faith (e.g., John 10:27-29; Rom. 8:30). Second Peter 2:18 says that by "speaking out arrogant words of vanity" false teachers "entice by fleshly desires, by sensuality, those who barely escape from the ones who live in error." The ones who are overturned are those who were looking for God, were wanting to believe, and were beginning to open up to the gospel. But then they came under false teaching, and it destroyed their weak, nonsaving faith. False religious systems wait to suck in the people who are looking for answers to the pains and pressures of life.

F. It Characterizes People Who Don't Belong to the Lord (v. 19)

1. The solid foundation (v. 19a)

Verse 19 says, "Nevertheless, the firm foundation of God stands." The firm foundation of God is the church—the redeemed. We are the true people of God who form the solid, immovable foundation that false teachers cannot uproot. False teachers will ruin some, shame some, lead some into ungodliness, corrupt some, and overturn the faith of some—but not the elect of God. We are a building not made with hands. We are the temple of the living God. We are the church Christ is building. The gates of hell will not prevail against us (Matt. 16:18). We are those who, having had a good work begun in us, will see it completed on the day of Jesus Christ (Phil. 1:6). We are those who will never be separated from the love of God in Christ (Rom. 8:35). We are those of whom Jesus said, "All that the Father gives Me shall come to Me. . . . that of all that He has given Me I lose nothing, but raise it up on the last day" (John 6:37, 39). False teaching may devastate the souls of many people, and it may confuse believers from time to time, but the foundation of the church of God in Christ is firm. First John 2:14 says, "You are strong, and the word of God abides in you, and you have overcome the evil one." God called out a people for salvation and eternal glory before the world began.

2. The guaranteed salvation (v. 19b)

Verse 19 says, "Having this seal." A seal was a mark of ownership, just as a builder put his name on the cornerstone to identify it as a building he built. We are the foundation of God—namely, His church. He has stamped us as belonging to Him.

a) Sovereign election

"The Lord knows those who are His."

The church can never be touched by false teachers, because we are His. He holds us in His sovereign power. We are His for eternity. The first seal we have is the seal of election. We are the elect. That seal is affixed to God's foundation. It guarantees permanence and makes dissolution impossible. In Matthew 7:22-23 the Lord says, "Many will say to Me on that day, 'Lord, Lord . . . .' And then I will declare to them, 'I never knew you; depart from Me, you who practice lawlessness.' " They cannot disturb the divine foundation. It will stand because we are the elect and the Lord knows who we are. Second Thessalonians 2:13 says, "God has chosen you from the beginning for salvation."

b) Personal sanctification

"Let everyone who names the name of the Lord abstain from wickedness."

To name the name of the Lord is to be identified with Him. If you belong to the Lord, abstain from wickedness. God's people are not only elect, but are also called to righteousness. God's election is an election to holiness. Our salvation is made up of God's predestining mercy and our inevitable duty. Paul said, "You have been bought with a price: therefore glorify God in your body" (1 Cor. 6:20). If we name the name of the Lord, we will abstain from wickedness. It is both an exhortation and an affirmation. The one who names the name of the Lord will not apostatize but will turn away from sin.

The two quotes in 2 Timothy 2:19 appear to be from Numbers 16. Korah rebelled against God, and many people joined him. But God judged them. Verse 5 says, "The Lord will show who is His." That is almost the same wording as the first statement in 2 Timothy 2:19: "The Lord knows those who are His." When Korah and his friends gathered against Moses and the rest of the people, Moses affirmed that the Lord knew who belonged to Him. The second statement in 2 Timothy 2:19 parallels Moses' command to the people in Numbers 16:26: "Depart now from the tents of these wicked men, and touch nothing that belongs to them."

God will come in judgment, but He knows whom He will spare because they belong to Him. We know who they are because they will depart from the tents of wickedness. From the divine side, they are elect; from the human side, they are obedient. All the false teaching Satan wants to bring across our path will avail nothing, because we stand firm on the foundation of God. Just as the rebellion under Korah ended in judgment, so will that of every false teacher.

Focusing on the Facts

1. Paul wanted Timothy to remind the true teachers of what (2 Tim. 2:14; see pp. 60-61)?
2. The leaders in the church at Ephesus were to perform their duty with what in mind (2 Tim. 2:14; see p. 61)?
3. Explain the two aspects of the presence of God (see pp. 62-63).
4. What solemn charge did Paul want Timothy to communicate to the leaders in Ephesus? Explain (see p. 64).
5. What has invaded the church through the false teachers? What kind of effect is it having on today's church (see p. 65)?
6. What does the future hold for those who listen to "word battles" (2 Tim. 2:14; see pp. 65-66)?
7. What is the key word of 2 Timothy 2:15? Why (see p. 66)?
8. What four things must believers do to avoid being teachers who will be ashamed before God? Explain each (see pp. 66-67).
9. Explain the literal meaning of the phrase "handling accurately" (see p. 67).
10. What principle is Paul teaching by the statement "handling accurately the word of truth" (see p. 68)?
11. What is the "word of truth" (see pp. 68-69)?
12. According to 2 Timothy 2:16, what are believers to avoid? Why (see p. 69)?
13. If people listen to false teachers, they will be led into what (2 Tim. 2:16; see p. 70)?
14. What error were Hymenaeus and Philetus propagating? Why is it a major error (2 Tim. 2:18; see pp. 70-71)?
15. Why did certain people have their faith overturned by listening to the error of the false teachers (see p. 71)?
16. What is the firm foundation of God (see p. 72)?
17. What are the two aspects of the seal God has put on us? Explain each (see pp. 72-73).

Pondering the Principles

1. Review the section on the presence of God (see pp. 62-64). Do you live as if God is the controlling factor on your life? Do you think of God as being present with you as you work at your job, drive in your car, go to the store, or relax in the evening? Some people think of God's presence only when they read the Bible or need something. Read Colossians 3:1-4. Begin to cultivate a mind that is preoccupied with heavenly things. Develop a God-consciousness. Take time to pray right now. Confess to God that you haven't given Him your attention. Begin today to commune with Him constantly throughout the day.

2. Read 2 Timothy 2:19. Spend some time meditating on the truths connected to God's seal on believers. What does it mean to you to know that you belong to God? Answer in the form of a prayer to God. What do you think Paul meant when he said believers should "abstain from wickedness"? How does that apply to you? Is there wickedness present in your life? If so, turn away from it. Confess it to God, and ask Him to help you to leave it behind.

Scripture Index

Topical Index